Doran

by Iain Gray

D0928450

Lang**Syne**

PUBLISHING

WRITING *to* REMEMBER

LangSyne

PUBLISHING

WRITING *to* REMEMBER

Vineyard Business Centre,
Pathhead, Midlothian EH37 5XP
Tel: 01875 321 203 Fax: 01875 321 233
E-mail: info@lang-syne.co.uk
www.langsyneshop.co.uk

Design by Dorothy Meikle
Printed by Montgomery Litho, Glasgow
© Lang Syne Publishers Ltd 2011

ISBN 978-1-85217-312-8

Doran

MOTTO:
Hope is the anchor of life.

CREST:
A lion's head atop a ducal coronet.

NAME variations include:
Ó Deoradhain (*Gaelic*)
Ó Deoráin (*Gaelic*)
O'Deoran
O'Doran
Dorain
Dorran
Dorrian

Chapter one:
Origins of Irish surnames

**According to an old saying, there are two types of Irish –
those who actually are Irish and those who wish they were.**

This sentiment is only one example of the allure that the
high romance and drama of the proud nation's history holds
for thousands of people scattered across the world today.

It's a sad fact, however, that the vast majority of Irish
surnames are found far beyond Irish shores, rather than on
the Emerald Isle itself.

The population stood at around eight million souls in
1841, but today it stands at fewer than six million.

This is mainly a tragic consequence of the potato
famine, also known as the Great Hunger, which devastated
Ireland between 1845 and 1849.

The Irish peasantry had become almost wholly reliant
for basic sustenance on the potato, first introduced from the
Americas in the seventeenth century.

When the crop was hit by a blight, at least 800,000
people starved to death while an estimated two million
others were forced to seek a new life far from their native
shores – particularly in America, Canada, and Australia.

The effects of the potato blight continued until about
1851, by which time a firm pattern of emigration had
become established.

Ireland's loss, however, was to the gain of the countries in which the immigrants settled, contributing enormously, as their descendants do today, to the well being of the nations in which their forefathers settled.

But those who were forced through dire circumstance to establish a new life in foreign parts never forgot their roots, or the proud heritage and traditions of the land that gave them birth.

Nor do their descendants.

It is a heritage that is inextricably bound up in the colourful variety of Irish names themselves – and the origin and history of these names forms an integral part of the vibrant drama that is the nation's history, one of both glorious fortune and tragic misfortune.

This history is well documented, and one of the most important and fascinating of the earliest sources are *The Annals of the Four Masters*, compiled between 1632 and 1636 by four friars at the Franciscan Monastery in County Donegal.

Compiled from earlier sources, and purporting to go back to the Biblical Deluge, much of the material takes in the mythological origins and history of Ireland and the Irish.

This includes tales of successive waves of invaders and settlers such as the Fomorians, the Partholonians, the Nemedians, the Fir Bolgs, the Tuatha De Danann, and the Laigain.

Of particular interest are the *Milesian Genealogies*,

because the majority of Irish clans today claim a descent from either Heremon, Ir, or Heber – three of the sons of Milesius, a king of what is now modern day Spain.

These sons invaded Ireland in the second millennium B.C, apparently in fulfilment of a mysterious prophecy received by their father.

This Milesian lineage is said to have ruled Ireland for nearly 3,000 years, until the island came under the sway of England's King Henry II in 1171 following what is known as the Cambro-Norman invasion.

This is an important date not only in Irish history in general, but for the effect the invasion subsequently had for Irish surnames.

'Cambro' comes from the Welsh, and 'Cambro-Norman' describes those Welsh knights of Norman origin who invaded Ireland.

But they were invaders who stayed, inter-marrying with the native Irish population and founding their own proud dynasties that bore Cambro-Norman names such as Archer, Barbour, Brannagh, Fitzgerald, Fitzgibbon, Fleming, Joyce, Plunkett, and Walsh – to name only a few.

These 'Cambro-Norman' surnames that still flourish throughout the world today form one of the three main categories in which Irish names can be placed – those of Gaelic-Irish, Cambro-Norman, and Anglo-Irish.

Previous to the Cambro-Norman invasion of the twelfth century, and throughout the earlier invasions and settlement of those wild bands of sea rovers known as the Vikings in the eighth and ninth centuries, the population of the island was relatively small, and it was normal for a person to be identified through the use of only a forename.

But as population gradually increased and there were many more people with the same forename, surnames were adopted to distinguish one person, or one community, from another.

Individuals identified themselves with their own particular tribe, or 'tuath', and this tribe – that also became known as a clann, or clan – took its name from some distinguished ancestor who had founded the clan.

The Gaelic-Irish form of the name Kelly, for example, is Ó Ceallaigh, or O'Kelly, indicating descent from an original 'Ceallaigh', with the 'O' denoting 'grandson of.' The name was later anglicised to Kelly.

The prefix 'Mac' or 'Mc', meanwhile, as with the clans of the Scottish Highlands, denotes 'son of.'

Although the Irish clans had much in common with their Scottish counterparts, one important difference lies in what are known as 'septs', or branches, of the clan.

Septs of Scottish clans were groups who often bore an entirely different name from the clan name but were under the clan's protection.

In Ireland, septs were groups that shared the same name and who could be found scattered throughout the four provinces of Ulster, Leinster, Munster, and Connacht.

The 'golden age' of the Gaelic-Irish clans, infused as their veins were with the blood of Celts, pre-dates the Viking invasions of the eighth and ninth centuries and the Norman invasion of the twelfth century, and the sacred heart of the country was the Hill of Tara, near the River Boyne, in County Meath.

Known in Gaelic as 'Teamhar na Rí', or Hill of Kings, it was the royal seat of the 'Ard Rí Éireann', or High King of Ireland, to whom the petty kings, or chieftains, from the island's provinces were ultimately subordinate.

It was on the Hill of Tara, beside a stone pillar known as the Irish 'Lia Fáil', or Stone of Destiny, that the High Kings were inaugurated and, according to legend, this stone would emit a piercing screech that could be heard all over Ireland when touched by the hand of the rightful king.

The Hill of Tara is today one of the island's main tourist attractions.

Opposition to English rule over Ireland, established in the wake of the Cambro-Norman invasion, broke out frequently and the harsh solution adopted by the powerful forces of the Crown was to forcibly evict the native Irish from their lands.

These lands were then granted to Protestant colonists, or 'planters', from Britain.

Many of these colonists, ironically, came from Scotland and were the descendants of the original 'Scotti', or 'Scots', who gave their name to Scotland after migrating there in the fifth century A.D., from the north of Ireland.

Colonisation entailed harsh penal laws being imposed on the majority of the native Irish population, stripping them practically of all of their rights.

The Crown's main bastion in Ireland was Dublin and its environs, known as the Pale, and it was the dispossessed peasantry who lived outside this Pale, desperately striving to eke out a meagre living.

It was this that gave rise to the modern-day expression of someone or something being 'beyond the pale'.

Attempts were made to stamp out all aspects of the ancient Gaelic-Irish culture, to the extent that even to bear a Gaelic-Irish name was to invite discrimination.

This is why many Gaelic-Irish names were anglicised with, for example, and noted above, Ó Ceallaigh, or O'Kelly, being anglicised to Kelly.

Succeeding centuries have seen strong revivals of Gaelic-Irish consciousness, however, and this has led to many families reverting back to the original form of their name, while the language itself is frequently found on the fluent tongues of an estimated 90,000 to 145,000 of the island's population.

Ireland's turbulent history of religious and political strife is one that lasted well into the twentieth century, a landmark century that saw the partition of the island into the twenty-six counties of the independent Republic of

Ireland, or Eire, and the six counties of Northern Ireland, or Ulster.

Dublin, originally founded by Vikings, is now a vibrant and truly cosmopolitan city while the proud city of Belfast is one of the jewels in the crown of Ulster.

It was Saint Patrick who first brought the light of Christianity to Ireland in the fifth century A.D.

Interpretations of this Christian message have varied over the centuries, often leading to bitter sectarian conflict – but the many intricately sculpted Celtic Crosses found all over the island are symbolic of a unity that crosses the sectarian divide.

It is an image that fuses the 'old gods' of the Celts with Christianity.

All the signs from the early years of this new millennium indicate that sectarian strife may soon become a thing of the past – with the Irish and their many kinsfolk across the world, be they Protestant or Catholic, finding common purpose in the rich tapestry of their shared heritage.

Chapter two:

Laying down the law

A clan with deep roots in the ancient soil of Ireland, the original territory of the Dorans is Leinster, which along with Ulster, Connacht, and Munster, is one of the island's four ancient provinces.

Bearers of the name are still to be found there to this day, although other septs of the family also flourish in the Northern Irish counties of Armagh and Down.

The Gaelic-Irish form of the name is Ó Deoradhain, or Ó Deoráin, and is thought to indicate 'wanderer', 'exile', or 'pilgrim', although some sources rather confusingly assert that it may stem from 'otter' or even a term indicating 'grief' or 'depression.'

But whatever the meaning, what is known for certain is that the Dorans, in all the rich variety of spellings of the name, were for centuries at the very heart of Ireland's turbulent affairs.

Their descent can be traced back through the dim mists of time from Heber, one of the island's earliest monarchs.

Along with Heremon, Ir, Amergin the Druid and four other brothers, he was a son of Milesius, a king of what is now modern day Spain, and who had planned to invade the Emerald Isle in fulfilment of a mysterious Druidic prophecy.

Milesius died before he could embark on the invasion but his sons, including Heber, Ir, Heremon and Amergin, successfully undertook the daunting task in his stead in about 1699 B.C.

Legend holds that their invasion fleet was scattered in a storm and Ir killed when his ship was driven onto the island of Scellig-Mhicheal, off the coast of modern day Co. Kerry.

Only Heremon, Heber, and Amergin survived, although Ir left issue.

Heremon and Heber became the first of the Milesian monarchs of Ireland, but Heremon later killed Heber in a quarrel said to have been caused by their wives, while Amergin was slain by Heremon in an argument over territory.

Along with the Dorans, other clans that trace a descent from Heber include those of Brady, Brennan, Carroll, O'Brien, O'Connor, O'Neill, and O'Sullivan.

The Dorans also, along with the O'Moores, O'Kellys, O'Devoys, O'Lalors, O'Dowlings, and McEvoys, later formed what was known as the celebrated Seven Septs of Leix, or Laois, also known today as Queen's County.

Under the leadership of the O'Moores, who trace their roots to the northern province of Ulster, the Seven Septs of Leix defended Leinster against the encroachment on the province of rival kings from Munster.

But while not on the field of battle, the Dorans pursued

the important calling of 'brehons', the name for Ireland's earliest lawmakers and judges.

'Brehon' stems from the Gaelic-Irish 'Breitheamh', meaning a judge, and the brehons were responsible for interpreting and dispensing justice based on a series of statutes that governed every aspect of daily life.

Also known as the Fenachas, or Law of the Feni, or freemen of Ireland, these laws were first written down during what is known as the Old Irish period of 600 to 900 A.D.

The laws show that Ireland was very far from being the backward and uncivilised nation so often depicted by its detractors.

Under the law known as *Cáin Adomnáin*, for example, first drawn up in 697 A.D., Irish women enjoyed a better status than that accorded any other women in Europe, with the right to seek divorce from abusive husbands and the right to hold their own property.

The position of brehon was hereditary, and the Dorans held the honoured position of hereditary brehons to the proud and powerful clan of Ó Murchada, or MacMurrough – later anglicised as Murphy.

Unfortunately for the Dorans, this close bond with the MacMurroughs was to have truly devastating consequences not only for themselves but also for other Gaelic-Irish clans.

The MacMurrough, or Murphy, name stemmed from Murchadh, a king of Leinster who was grandfather to the famous, although some would describe him as infamous, Dermot MacMurrough.

This mighty warrior king of Leinster holds the dubious distinction of having paved the path for the twelfth century Cambro-Norman invasion of Ireland and its subsequent domination by the English.

Twelfth century Ireland was far from being a unified nation, split up as it was into territories ruled over by squabbling chieftains such as MacMurrough, who ruled as kings in their own right – and this inter-clan rivalry worked to the advantage of the invaders.

In a series of bloody conflicts one chieftain, or king, would occasionally gain the upper hand over his rivals, and by 1156 the most powerful was Muirchertach MacLochlainn, king of the powerful O'Neills.

The equally powerful Rory O'Connor, king of the province of Connacht, opposed him, but MacLochlainn increased his power and influence by allying himself with MacMurrough.

MacLochlainn and MacMurrough were aware that the main key to the kingdom of Ireland was the thriving trading port of Dublin that had been established by invading Vikings, or Ostmen, in 852 A.D.

Their combined forces took Dublin, but when MacLochlainn died the Dubliners rose up in revolt and overthrew the unpopular MacMurrough.

There had certainly been no love lost between

MacMurrough and the Dubliners – who had not only killed his father but as an added insult buried his corpse beside that of a dead dog.

A triumphant Rory O'Connor entered Dublin and was later inaugurated as Ard Rí, but MacMurrough was not one to humbly accept defeat.

He appealed for help from England's Henry II in unseating O'Connor, an act that was to radically affect the future course of Ireland's fortunes.

The English monarch agreed to help MacMurrough, but distanced himself from direct action by delegating his Norman subjects in Wales with the task.

These ambitious and battle-hardened barons and knights had first settled in Wales following the Norman Conquest of England in 1066 and, with an eye on rich booty, plunder, and lands, were only too eager to obey their sovereign's wishes and furnish MacMurrough with aid.

He crossed the Irish Sea to Bristol, where he rallied powerful barons such as Robert Fitzstephen and Maurice Fitzgerald to his cause, along with Gilbert de Clare, Earl of Pembroke, also known as Strongbow.

As an inducement to Strongbow, MacMurrough offered him the hand of his beautiful young daughter, Aife, in marriage, with the further sweetener to the deal that he would take over the province of Leinster, home to not only his own clan but also the Dorans, on MacMurrough's death.

The mighty Norman war machine moved into action in

1169, and so fierce and disciplined was their onslaught on the forces of O'Connor and his allies that by 1171 they had re-captured Dublin, in the name of MacMurrough, and other strategically important territories.

Henry II now began to take cold feet over the venture, realising that he may have created a rival in the form of a separate Norman kingdom in Ireland.

Accordingly, he landed on the island, near Waterford, at the head of a large army and with the aim of curbing the power of his barons.

But protracted war was averted when the barons submitted to the royal will, promising homage and allegiance in return for holding the territories they had conquered in the king's name.

Henry also received the submission and homage of many of the Irish chieftains, tired as they were with internecine warfare and also perhaps realising that as long as they were rivals and not united they were no match for the powerful forces the English Crown could muster.

English dominion over Ireland was ratified through the Treaty of Windsor of 1175, under the terms of which Rory O'Connor, for example, was allowed to rule territory unoccupied by the Normans in the role of a vassal of the king.

It is also perhaps rather bitterly ironic that Henry II was also of Milesian descent – this was through his mother Maude, who was descended from the Scottish monarch

Fergus Mor MacEarca, who traced his descent from Heremon.

Dermot MacMurrough had died only a few months before Henry landed in Ireland.

His unfortunate legacy is to have opened the door to not only the Cambro-Norman invaders but also to further waves of Anglo-Norman adventurers who, over succeeding centuries, acquired territories at the expense of the Gaelic-Irish such as the Dorans.

Chapter three:

In freedom's cause

One indication of the trials and tribulations suffered by the Gaelic-Irish can be found in a desperate plea sent to Pope John XII by Roderick O'Carroll of Ely, Donald O'Neill of Ulster, and a number of other Irish chieftains in 1318.

They stated: 'As it very constantly happens, whenever an Englishman, by perfidy or craft, kills an Irishman, however noble, or however innocent, be he clergy or layman, there is no penalty or correction enforced against the person who may be guilty of such wicked murder.

'But rather the more eminent the person killed and the higher rank which he holds among his own people, so much more is the murderer honoured and rewarded by the English, and not merely by the people at large, but also by the religious and bishops of the English race.'

This appeal to the Pope had little effect on what became the increasingly harsh policy of the occupying English Crown against the native Irish such as the Dorans and rebellion was endemic.

By the mid-sixteenth century the Dorans were accused of harbouring rebels, with one contemporary source stating that they were "succouring rebellious plunderers in their judicial capacity."

At this time the main seat of the Dorans was at Chappell, in present day Co. Wexford, in an area of what was then virtual wilderness.

But by only a few decades later, and despite English doubts over where their true sympathies lay, they were being consulted on matters of Irish law by no less a powerful figure than the Crown-appointed Lord Deputy of Ireland.

Another indication of how well established they had become, walking a tightrope between the demands of the Crown and struggling to defend their ancient rights and privileges, is that they gave their name to the township of Doransland.

But while the family continued to flourish in Co. Wexford, leading members of the sept found their fortunes in radical decline.

Discontent had grown on the island over the policy known as 'plantation', or settlement of loyal Protestants on lands previously held by the native Irish.

This policy had started during the reign from 1491 to 1547 of Henry VIII, whose Reformation effectively outlawed the established Roman Catholic faith throughout his dominions, and continued throughout the subsequent reigns of Elizabeth I, James I, Charles I, and in the aftermath of the Cromwellian invasion of the island in 1649.

Rebellion erupted in 1594 in the form of what became Cogadh na Naoi mBliama, or the Nine Years War, with a whirlwind of devastation wreaked on English settlements and garrisons in a daring series of lightning raids.

In 1596 a rebel army led by Hugh O'Neill, 2nd Earl of Tyrone, and Red Hugh O'Donnell, defeated an English army at the battle of Clontibert, while in August of 1598 another significant defeat was inflicted at the battle of Yellow Ford.

As English control over Ireland teetered on the brink of collapse, thousands more troops, including mercenaries, were hastily despatched to the island and, in the face of the overwhelming odds against them, Red Hugh and the Earl of Tyrone sought help from England's enemy, Spain.

A well-equipped Spanish army under General del Aquila landed at Kinsale in December of 1601, but was forced into surrender only a few weeks later, in January of 1602.

Resistance continued until 1603, but proved abortive.

Four years later, in September of 1607 and in what is known as The Flight of the Earls, Hugh O'Neill and Rory O'Donnell, 1st Earl of Tyrconnel, sailed into foreign exile from the village of Rathmullan, on the shore of Lough Swilly, in Co. Donegal, accompanied by ninety loyal followers.

This event is seen as having heralded the final collapse of the ancient Gaelic Order of clans such as the Dorans.

By 1609 leading members of the Doran sept were 'transplanted' to Co. Kerry, where many of the name can be found to this day.

It was also at this period that another sept became established further north in the present day counties of Armagh and Down – where the common form of the name is Dorrian.

One distinguished member of this sept was the Most Reverend Patrick Dorrian, born in 1814 and who died in 1885 and who served as the Bishop of Down and Connor.

Following the Nine Years War Ireland was devastated by a further series of rebellions, most notably a revolt that broke out in 1641 and ended in the aftermath of the murderous Cromwellian invasion of 1649.

There was also an abortive Jacobite Rising from 1688 to 1691 on behalf of the deposed Stuart monarch James II, while a short-lived rebellion erupted in 1798 in a bid to restore Irish freedom and independence.

The roots of this Rising are complex, but in essence it was sparked off by a fusion of sectarian and agrarian unrest and a burning desire for political reform that had been shaped by the French revolutionary slogan of 'liberty, equality, and fraternity.'

A movement had come into existence that embraced middle-class intellectuals and the oppressed peasantry, and if this loosely bound movement could be said to have had a leader, it was Wolfe Tone, a Protestant from Kildare and leading light of a radical republican movement known as the United Irishmen.

Despite attempts by the British government to concede

a degree of agrarian and political reform, it was a case of far too little and much too late, and by 1795 the United Irishmen, through Wolfe Tone, were receiving help from France – Britain's enemy.

A French invasion fleet was despatched to Ireland in December of 1796, but scattered by storms off Bantry Bay.

Two years later, in the summer of 1798, rebellion broke out – the first flames of revolt being fanned in Ulster, but soon dying out, only to be replaced by a much more serious conflagration centred mainly in the Doran territory of Co. Wexford.

Rebel victory was achieved at the battle of Oulart Hill, followed by another victory at the battle of Three Rocks, but the peasant army was no match for the 20,000 troops or so that descended on Wexford.

Defeat followed at the battle of Vinegar Hill on 21 June, followed by another decisive defeat at Kilcumney Hill five days later.

An Act of Union between Great Britain and Ireland was passed in 1800, and this later served to fuel the flames of further revolt – and one of the leading rebel organisers was Charles Gilfoyle Doran, born in 1835 in Dunlavin, in Co. Cork.

Trained as a civil engineer he found employment with a firm of architects, and in 1866 was given the trusted and responsible role of Clerk of Works for the building of a new cathedral at Queenstown, also known as Cobh.

But unknown to only a select few at the time, Doran was a member of the Republican movement known as the Fenian Brotherhood, also known as the Irish Republican Brotherhood, or IRB.

His job as Clerk of Works meant that he had to travel frequently throughout Ireland, and he used this as a cover to plot and organise subversive activities.

Following a brief and abortive Fenian Rising in 1867 Doran, fearing arrest and imprisonment, fled to France for a time, but returned to resume his work on Cobh Cathedral and his clandestine Republican activities.

Later a member of the Supreme Council of the IRB he was responsible, along with Thomas Nelson Underwood, for the transformation of the movement into a more effective instrument for the achievement of eventual liberation of Ireland from Union with England.

In addition to his Republican activities Doran, who died in 1909, was also a gifted antiquarian and writer.

The author of several important historical works, including a history of Co. Cork and Cork City, he also had in his care only one of three manuscript copies of the rare and precious *Tripartite Life of St. Patrick* – that had been passed down through generations of Dorans.

Chapter four:

On the world stage

Bearers of the Doran name have gained distinction in a wide range of endeavours.

Born in 1911 in Amarillo, Texas, **Ann Doran** was the American actress who, by the time of her death in 2000, had appeared in more than 500 films and more than 1,000 television shows.

She first took to the stage at the tender age of four, appearing in silent films under assumed names so that her father's disapproving family would not find out about their grand-daughter's acting career.

Signed to Columbia Pictures in 1938, she appeared in a host of film serials that included *The Spider's Web* and *Flying G-Men*, in addition to B-movie features such as *Five Little Peppers*.

Leading roles followed in the *Charley Chase* comedies and the *Rusty* series in 1945.

One of her most memorable roles was as the domineering mother of James Dean's character in the 1955 *Rebel Without A Cause* – while during the making of the movie she became a close friend of the troubled and much younger actor.

Also on stage **Matthew J. Doran**, born in 1976 in Sydney, is the Australian actor who appeared in the popular television soap *Home and Away* from 1992 to 1996, but who has also appeared in movies that include the 1999 *The Matrix*, in the role of 'Mouse', *The Thin Red Line*, from 1998, *Stars Wars Episode II: Attack of the Clones*, from 2002, and the 2006 *Macbeth*.

In the world of music **Chris Doran**, born in 1979 and from Waterford, is the Irish pop star who represented his native Republic of Ireland at the 2004 Eurovision Song Contest in Istanbul, Turkey.

Although not the winner of the contest his song, *If My World Stopped Turning*, became a hit, along with subsequent songs including *Nothing's Gonna Change My Love For You* and *Hey Girl*.

Recognised as having been one of Ireland's greatest traditional musicians, **Johnny Doran** was the skilled player of the Irish uilleann pipes who was born into a travelling family at Rathnew, Co. Wicklow, in 1907.

He came from a long and distinguished line of exponents of traditional music and, by the age of 20, he was touring the length and breadth of the island in a horse-drawn cart, playing at fairs, horse races, and other sporting events.

Tragedy struck when he was aged 41, when he was paralysed from the waist down after a brick wall collapsed on top of his caravan while it was parked in Dublin's Cornmarket area.

He died two years later in Athy, in Co. Kildare, and is buried in Rathnew Cemetery.

Only a year before his accident his friend John Kelly, a fiddle player, had persuaded Doran to record a selection of his playing on acetate disc under the auspice of the Irish Folklore Commission.

The recordings were a great success and remain an important and highly treasured legacy.

Dorans have also excelled, and continue to excel, in the highly competitive world of sport.

Born in 1963 in St. Louis, Missouri, **Daryl Doran** is the retired American indoor soccer player who, at the time of writing, holds the record for having played the most games – 827 – in the sport's history.

Now involved in coaching, teams he played for included the St. Louis Steamers, St. Louis Ambush, and the Los Angeles Lazers.

Born Thomas J. Doran in 1880 in Westchester County, New York, **Long Tom Doran** was the Major League Baseball back-up catcher who enjoyed a highly successful career from 1904 to 1906 playing for teams that included the Boston Americans and Detroit Tigers.

He died in 1910.

Also in baseball William Doran, born in 1958 in Cincinnati, Ohio, is the former Major League baseman and now top coach who played from 1982 to 1993 with teams that included the Houston Astros, Cincinnati Reds, and Milwaukee Brewers.

In the rough and tumble but nevertheless skilled game of

hurling, **Tony Doran** is the former player who was born in 1946 in Boolanogue, Co. Wexford.

The recipient of a number of All-Ireland titles, including his first All-Ireland medal when he was aged 20, he played mainly for his home county.

On the cricket pitch **Daniel Doran**, born in 1981 in Hobart, Tasmania is the talented Australian bowler who, at the time of writing, plays for the Queensland Bulls.

Also in Australia Mark Dolan, born in 1970, is the sports journalist and radio and television commentator better known by his nickname of 'Ferret.'

In the ecclesiastical sphere Bishop Thomas G. Doran, born in 136 in Rockford, Illinois, and who was ordained a priest in 1936 is, at the time of writing, the 8th Roman Catholic Bishop for the Rockford diocese.

In the world of art **Juno Doran**, born in 1966 in Abrantes, Portugal is the contemporary visual artist who first came to international attention in the late 1990s for her photo-realist portrait paintings.

Now based in London, she exhibits throughout the world.

Born in 1968 **Colleen Doran** is the American comic book writer and artist best known for her *A Distant Soil* fantasy series. She was aged five when she won an art contest sponsored by the Walt Disney Company, and aged only 15 when she received her first professional assignment for a leading advertising agency.

In the world of literature John Doran was the author of Irish parentage who was born in London in 1807.

A tutor to the sons and daughters of some of Britain's most distinguished families, he travelled widely on the Continent and later contributed journalistic sketches to *The Literary Chronicle*, forerunner of the famed literary magazine *The Atheneum*.

He translated works into English by French, German, and Italian authors while his own books include the 1856 *Table Traits and Habits of Men*, and *Memoirs of our Great Towns*, published in the same year as his death in 1878.

Born in 1905, **Madeleine Doran** was the leading American poet and literary critic whose collections of works include *Something About Swans*, published in 1973, and the 1974 *Time's Foot*.

She died in 1996.

In the often cut-throat world of politics **Frank Doran** is the Scottish Labour MP who was born in 1949 in Edinburgh.

The partner of fellow Labour MP Joan Ruddock, he was first elected to the British House of Commons in 1987 for the Aberdeen South constituency and served as his party's opposition frontbench spokesman on energy.

Defeated in the 1992 election, he was re-elected in 1997 for the new constituency of Aberdeen Central and was appointed parliamentary private Secretary to the Minister of State at the Department of Trade and Industry.

The Aberdeen Central seat was abolished in 2005 following changes to electoral boundaries, but Doran was elected to the Aberdeen North seat.

At the time of writing he serves as Treasurer of the All-Party Oil and Gas Group.

On the high seas **Admiral Walter F. Doran**, born in 1945 in Albany, New York, is the retired U.S. Navy Admiral who served from 2002 to 2005 as Commander in Chief, Unites States Pacific Fleet.

Commissioned as an Ensign in 1967, he had achieved Flag rank by 1993 and served on the staff of the Chief of Naval Operations and as assistant to the chairman of Joints Chief of Staff.

His many honours include the Distinguished Service Medal, the Legion of Merit, and the Navy and Marine Corps Commendation Medal.

Also at sea **John James Doran**, born in Boston, Massachusetts in 1862 and who died in 1904, was the sailor in the United Sates Navy during the Spanish-American War of 1898 who received the Medal of Honour for his bravery under fire during a naval action off Cuba in May of that year.

Two ships, *USS Doran*, have been named in his honour.

'Doran' is also a place name in both Dublin and Minnesota, while Ben Doran is a mountain in Scotland.

Key dates in Ireland's history from the first settlers to the formation of the Irish Republic:

circa 7000 B.C.	Arrival and settlement of Stone Age people.
circa 3000 B.C.	Arrival of settlers of New Stone Age period.
circa 600 B.C.	First arrival of the Celts.
200 A.D.	Establishment of Hill of Tara, Co. Meath, as seat of the High Kings.
circa 432 A.D.	Christian mission of St. Patrick.
800-920 A.D.	Invasion and subsequent settlement of Vikings.
1002 A.D.	Brian Boru recognised as High King.
1014	Brian Boru killed at battle of Clontarf.
1169-1170	Cambro-Norman invasion of the island.
1171	Henry II claims Ireland for the English Crown.
1366	Statutes of Kilkenny ban marriage between native Irish and English.
1529-1536	England's Henry VIII embarks on religious Reformation.
1536	Earl of Kildare rebels against the Crown.
1541	Henry VIII declared King of Ireland.
1558	Accession to English throne of Elizabeth I.
1565	Battle of Affane.
1569-1573	First Desmond Rebellion.
1579-1583	Second Desmond Rebellion.
1594-1603	Nine Years War.
1606	Plantation' of Scottish and English settlers.
1607	Flight of the Earls.
1632-1636	Annals of the Four Masters compiled.
1641	Rebellion over policy of plantation and other grievances.
1649	Beginning of Cromwellian conquest.
1688	Flight into exile in France of Catholic Stuart monarch James II as Protestant Prince William of Orange invited to take throne of England along with his wife, Mary.
1689	William and Mary enthroned as joint monarchs; siege of Derry.
1690	Jacobite forces of James defeated by William at battle of the Boyne (July) and Dublin taken.

1691	Athlone taken by William; Jacobite defeats follow at Aughrim, Galway, and Limerick; conflict ends with Treaty of Limerick (October) and Irish officers allowed to leave for France.
1695	Penal laws introduced to restrict rights of Catholics; banishment of Catholic clergy.
1704	Laws introduced constricting rights of Catholics in landholding and public office.
1728	Franchise removed from Catholics.
1791	Foundation of United Irishmen republican movement.
1796	French invasion force lands in Bantry Bay.
1798	Defeat of Rising in Wexford and death of United Irishmen leaders Wolfe Tone and Lord Edward Fitzgerald.
1800	Act of Union between England and Ireland.
1803	Dublin Rising under Robert Emmet.
1829	Catholics allowed to sit in Parliament.
1845-1849	The Great Hunger: thousands starve to death as potato crop fails and thousands more emigrate.
1856	Phoenix Society founded.
1858	Irish Republican Brotherhood established.
1873	Foundation of Home Rule League.
1893	Foundation of Gaelic League.
1904	Foundation of Irish Reform Association.
1913	Dublin strikes and lockout.
1916	Easter Rising in Dublin and proclamation of an Irish Republic.
1917	Irish Parliament formed after Sinn Fein election victory.
1919-1921	War between Irish Republican Army and British Army.
1922	Irish Free State founded, while six northern counties remain part of United Kingdom as Northern Ireland, or Ulster; civil war up until 1923 between rival republican groups.
1949	Foundation of Irish Republic after all remaining constitutional links with Britain are severed.